Steck-Vaughn
Shutterbug Books
SOCIAL STUDIES

Totem Story

by Abby Jackson

STECK-VAUGHN
Harcourt Supplemental Publishers

www.steck-vaughn.com

How can you tell a story without words?
Some Native Americans tell stories with totem poles.

Totem poles are tall wooden poles carved from trees.

People and animals are carved on the poles.

Each carving stands for part of a story.

3

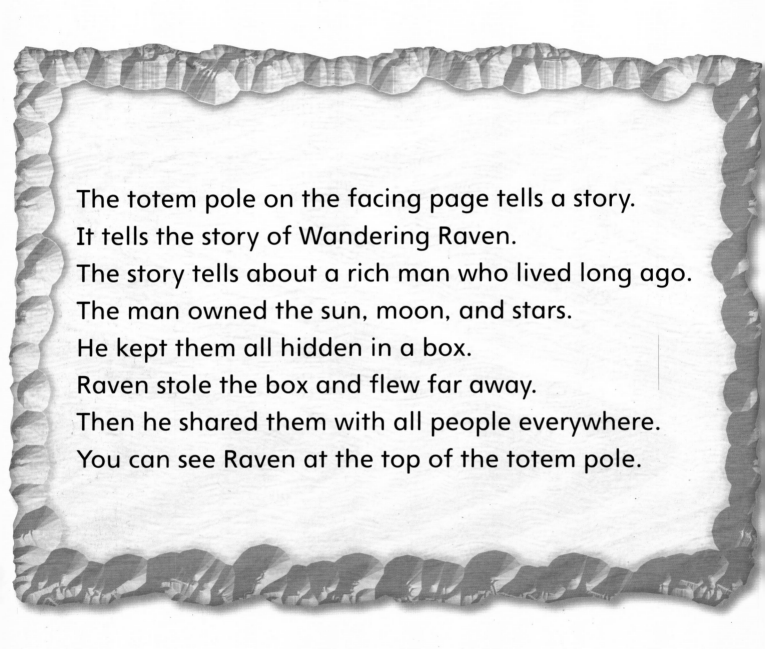

The totem pole on the facing page tells a story.

It tells the story of Wandering Raven.

The story tells about a rich man who lived long ago.

The man owned the sun, moon, and stars.

He kept them all hidden in a box.

Raven stole the box and flew far away.

Then he shared them with all people everywhere.

You can see Raven at the top of the totem pole.

Not all totem poles tell stories about animals.
Some totem poles are built for other reasons.

Totem poles can tell about a family, or clan.
These poles may be part of the clan house.

Most totem poles are placed outside.

Some stand high above the treetops.

They are placed where visitors can see them.

Long ago, many Native Americans traveled by canoe.

Totem poles were placed facing the water.

People would see them as they came to shore.

Today many people travel by car.

So now, many totem poles face the road.

Totem poles begin as tall cedar trees.

These trees are very special to totem pole carvers.

Carvers thank the trees for becoming totem poles.

Native Americans use special tools to carve totem poles.
Fathers teach their children how to use the tools.
It takes many years to learn.

After they are carved, most totem poles are painted.
Long ago, Native Americans made their own paint.
They made paint from fish eggs, rocks, and plants.

It takes a very long time to make a totem pole.

It can take a whole year to make just one.

Many people work together to raise the pole into place.

Putting up a new totem pole is an important event.
It is a time for Native Americans to celebrate their culture.

The celebration of a new totem pole can last for days.
There is food, music, and dancing.

Totem stories can be fun for everyone.
What story might this totem pole tell?